FROM HANON TO JAZZ

SKILLS, ETUDES, & PERFORMANCE PIECES
A Companion to Traditional Keyboard Instruction

by Dr. Bert Konowitz

Production: Frank and Gail Hackinson
Production Coordinator: Derek Richard
Editor: Edwin McLean
Cover: Terpstra Design, San Francisco
Engraving: Tempo Music Press, Inc.
Printer: Tempo Music Press, Inc.

THE
F·J·H
MUSIC
COMPANY
INC.
Frank J. Hackinson

ISBN-13: 978-1-56939-296-6

Table of Contents

Part 3: Basic Jazz Repertoire— The Standards

Conversation Between
C.L. Hanon (20th century)*
and Bert Konowitz (21st century)

Hanon: The study of the piano is nowadays so general, and good pianists are so numerous, that mediocrity on this instrument is no longer endured. As a result, I have written *The Virtuoso Pianist,* consisting of 60 exercises.

Konowitz: In a similar manner, there are so many classical teachers and students who yearn to perform the styles and sounds of jazz, America's classical music. It is for them that I have created *From Hanon to Jazz,* consisting of instructional études and performance pieces.

Hanon: Good. In my book, there are exercises necessary for acquiring agility, independence, strength, and perfect evenness of fingers—all indispensable qualities for fine execution.

Konowitz: Your approach, Mr. Hanon, has worked beautifully for so many pianists over the years that I have decided to **begin** with your exercise patterns to learn how to play jazz!

Hanon: Did you use my approach to 5-finger patterns, scales, and arpeggios, which pianists have loved through the years?

Konowitz: Absolutely. We begin by playing Hanon-type 5-finger patterns, adding a variety of **jazz accents** as the **blues scale** is introduced.

Hanon: In *The Virtuoso Pianist,* I not only emphasized 5-finger patterns, but stressed scales, arpeggios, and their varied combinations. It was my aim to unite in one work special exercises that render possible a complete course of pianistic study.

Konowitz: *From Hanon to Jazz* is created using your concept of a complete approach. The section on the techniques of developing jazz **hands** also includes L.H. accompaniments, such as **boogie bass, comping,** and **contemporary swing bass.**

Hanon: But, what about my idea of a complete course of pianistic study?

Konowitz: You are absolutely correct, Mr. Hanon. In addition to fine execution, learning to play jazz also requires that you learn how to use your **eyes**, such as knowing how to read chord and slash chord symbols as you develop melodies and play **standards** from a **Fake Book**. It's all here in one book—now, that's what I call complete!

Hanon: My book is intended for all piano pupils. It may be taken up after the pupil has studied about a year. More advanced students will study it and apply a range of creative ideas, such as using varied dynamics, tempos, and rhythms.

*Mr. Hanon's comments are adapted from the Preface to his famous book The Virtuoso Pianist *(FJH H1006).*

Konowitz: This is exactly what I do in *From Hanon to Jazz*. However, ever since you wrote your book over a hundred years ago, most pianists nowadays expect that skills gained from **exercises** (études) will be applied to exciting performance pieces. That's why all my études are followed by fun-to-play pieces.

Hanon and Konowitz: (They smile approvingly at each other and shake hands.) Perfect! OK, everyone, let's get going and learn to play jazz.

Before You Begin

This book will offer success to all of the following:

1. Classical music students and teachers who have always wished that they could learn to play in the jazz style, but assumed that it was something one could not learn

2. Classical music students and teachers who did not know how to use traditional skills, such as the Hanon exercises, as an easy bridge to learning how to play in the jazz style

3. Classical music students and teachers who have always wished that they could learn to play chords and create melodies by reading chord symbols

4. Classical music students and teachers who have always wished to learn how to play basic jazz repertoire (standards) from a Fake Book

This text has been carefully crafted from an instructional design that reflects the need to "begin at the beginning," slowly building fundamental musical concepts that will result in enriched performing skills and knowledge.

You will learn the unique techniques of jazz Hands, Eyes, and Performance— as you discover that learning to play jazz is a perfect companion to traditional keyboard instruction.

Performing Jazz:

Jazz Eighth Notes—They are played unevenly as follows:

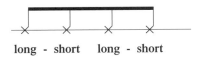

long - short   long - short

Jazz Accents—Play the accents lightly. After they are introduced in Part I, you are invited to use your musical judgment to decide when and where they will be used.

Jazz Touch—Play in a slightly detached manner, as you would a Bach piece.

Recording Application—All the recorded pieces are presented at an easy-to-play tempo. Track numbers are printed in the following manner: **17**

Part 1: Jazz Hands

From Hanon 5-finger pattern to jazz

Warm-up practice sequence

Step 1: Hanon pattern No. 1*

Step 2: Basic jazz accents

Step 3: 5-finger blues scale

from The Virtuoso Pianist

Basic Jazz Accents Étude No. 1

Focus

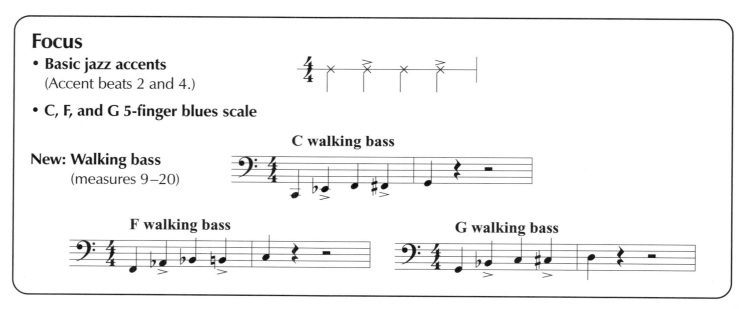

- **Basic jazz accents**
  (Accent beats 2 and 4.)

- **C, F, and G 5-finger blues scale**

New: Walking bass
  (measures 9–20)

C walking bass

F walking bass

G walking bass

Hangin' Out

Easy swing (♩ = ca. 84)

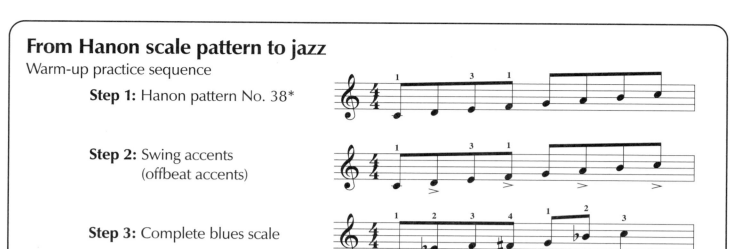

From Hanon scale pattern to jazz
Warm-up practice sequence

Step 1: Hanon pattern No. 38*

Step 2: Swing accents
    (offbeat accents)

Step 3: Complete blues scale

*from The Virtuoso Pianist

Swing Accents Étude No. 2

Moderate swing (♩ = ca. 76-104)

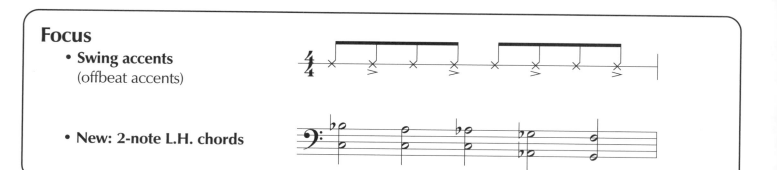

Focus
- **Swing accents**
  (offbeat accents)

- **New: 2-note L.H. chords**

Good Job!

Relaxed swing (♩ = ca. 84-96)

14

Combining basic jazz and swing accents

R.H. warm-up sequence
Step 1: Basic jazz accents

Step 2: Swing accents

Step 3: Combination of basic and swing accents

Combining Basic Jazz and Swing Accents Étude No. 3

($\quad$ = ca. 60-88)

Adding a L.H. comp* pattern

Warm-up

*accompaniment

Combining Basic Jazz and Swing Accents Étude No. 3A

($\quad$ = ca. 76-96)

Focus

• **This piece combines basic accents with swing accents…**

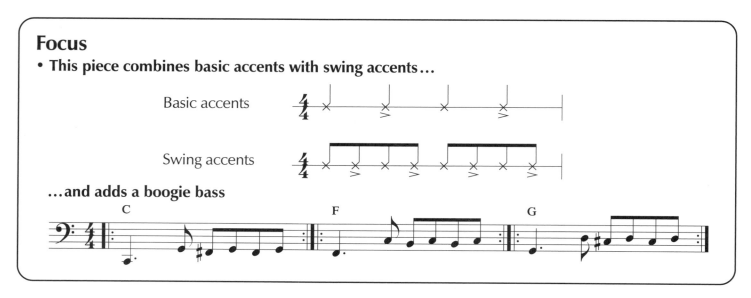

Basic accents

Swing accents

…and adds a boogie bass

The Shining Light Blues

Medium swing (♩ = ca. 104)

mf

f

From Hanon arpeggio to jazz phrasing

Warm-up practice sequence

Step 1: Hanon pattern No. 41*

Step 2: Jazz phrasing (Accent the end of the phrase.)

Step 3: Arpeggio type, combined with blues scale

*from The Virtuoso Pianist

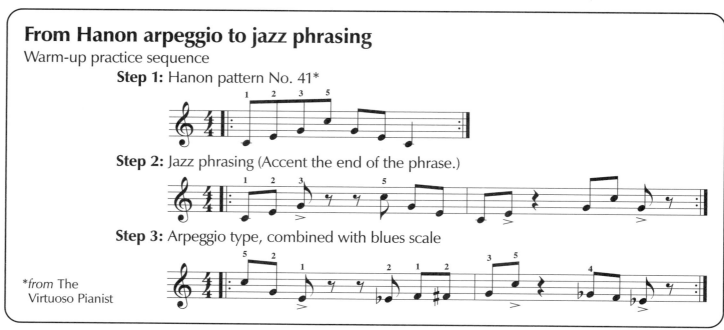

Jazz Phrasing Étude No. 4

Easy swing (♩ = ca. 76-96)

Focus

- **Jazz phrasing**
  (Accent the end of the phrase.)

- **New: Swing bass**
  (contemporary)

Walk-Around-the-Block Blues

Medium bright swing ($\quad$ = ca. 104)

Part 2: Jazz Eyes

Learning To Read Chord Symbols and Lead Sheets
Major and Minor Chords

Major chords

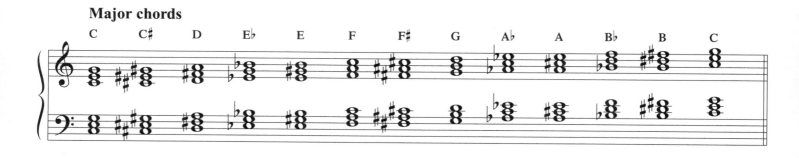

Minor chords

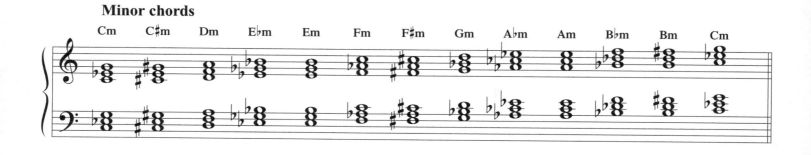

Lead sheet—Melody with chord symbols written above the staff.

Actual performance of the lead sheet

From lead sheet to performance

Warm-up practice sequence

Step 1: Play chords as written.

Step 2: Play chords in rhythm.

Step 3: Play *Lead Sheet Étude No. 1* using Step 2 rhythms.

Step 4: Compare your performance to actual notation below.

Lead Sheet Étude No. 1

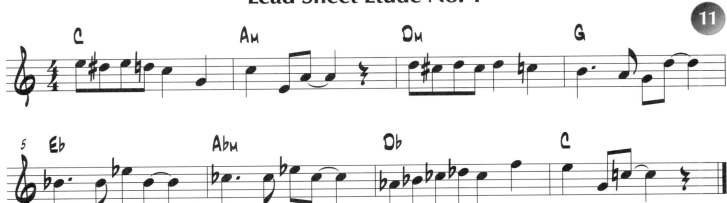

Actual notation of *Lead Sheet Étude No. 1*

Moderate swing (♩ = ca. 106)

24

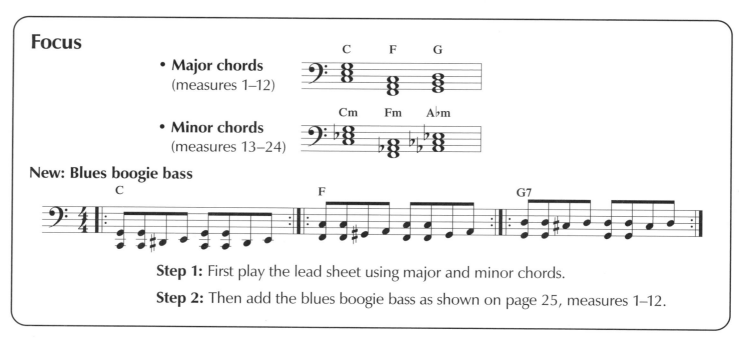

Focus

- **Major chords** (measures 1–12)
- **Minor chords** (measures 13–24)

New: Blues boogie bass

Step 1: First play the lead sheet using major and minor chords.

Step 2: Then add the blues boogie bass as shown on page 25, measures 1–12.

Movin', That's What I Said, Movin'

Moderate swing (♩ = ca. 108)

N.C.—"No Chord"; stop playing L.H. until next chord appears.

Realization of Movin', That's What I Said, Movin'

Moderate swing (♩ = ca. 108)

Learning To Read 7th Chord Symbols

Major 7th Chords

Scale steps: 1   2   3   4   5   6   7

Cmaj7 Dmaj7 Emaj7 Fmaj7 Gmaj7 Amaj7 Bmaj7 Cmaj7

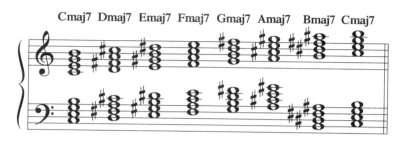

Dominant 7th Chords

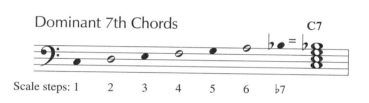

Scale steps: 1   2   3   4   5   6   ♭7

C7   D7   E7   F7   G7   A7   B7   C7

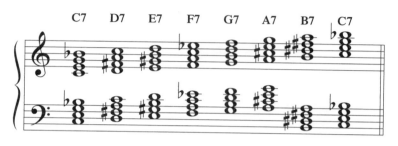

Minor 7th Chords

Scale steps: 1   2   ♭3   4   5   6   ♭7

Cm7 Dm7 Em7 Fm7 Gm7 Am7 Bm7 Cm7

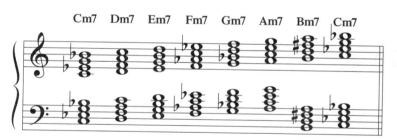

Write & Play

Write the L.H. chords in the bass clef below.
Use half notes on beats 1 and 3.

From lead sheet to performance

Warm-up practice sequence

Step 1: Play chords as written.

Step 2: Play chords in rhythm.

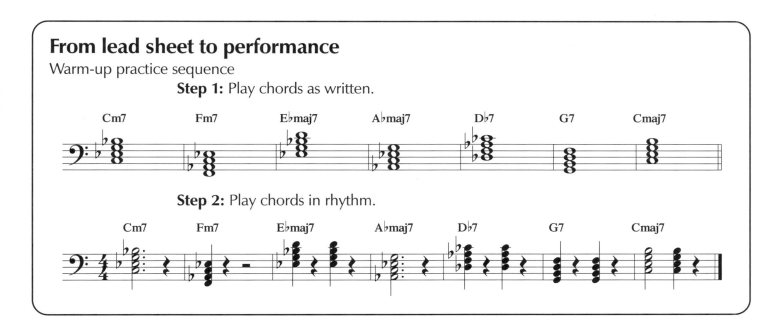

Lead Sheet Étude No. 2

Actual notation of *Lead Sheet Étude No. 2*

Write & Play

Write the L.H. chords in the bass clef, using the chord symbols as a guide.
Then play the lead sheet melody with the chords.

Easy Ride

Slow swing (♩ = ca. 88-104)

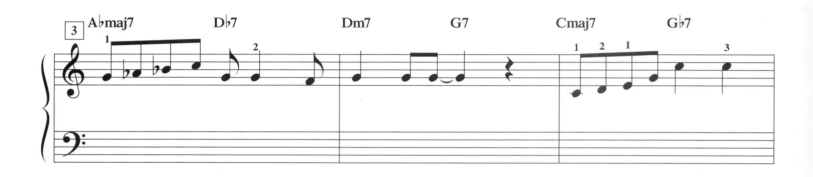

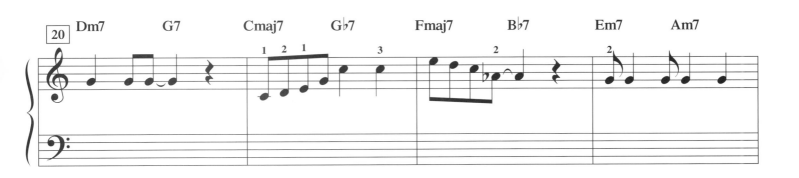

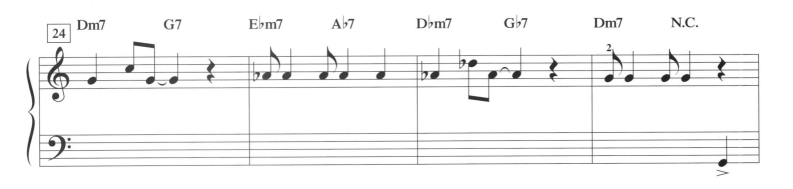

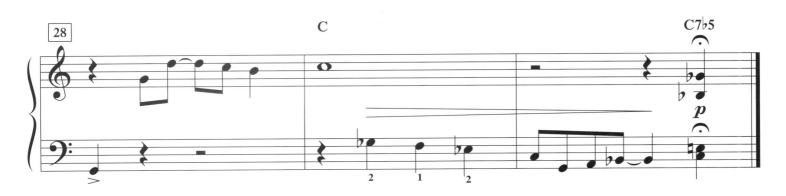

From Chord Symbols to Chord-Tone Melody

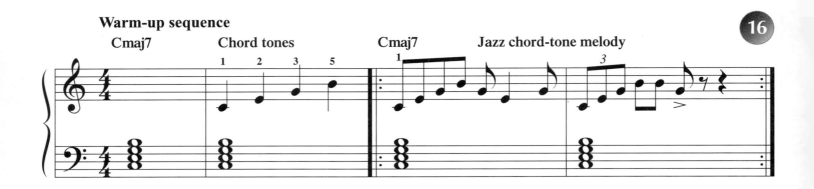

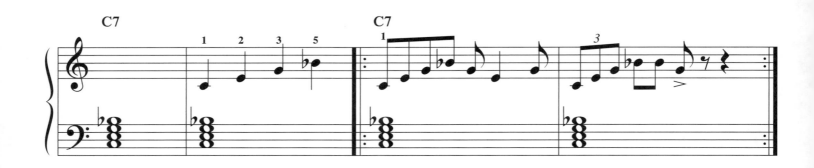

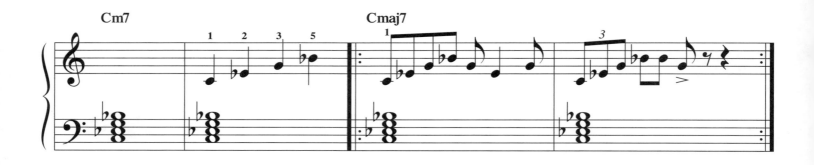

From chord symbols to chord-tone melody

Étude No. 3

Focus

- ### Cm(maj7) chords, chord-tone melody
  This chord is a minor triad with a major 7th above the root.

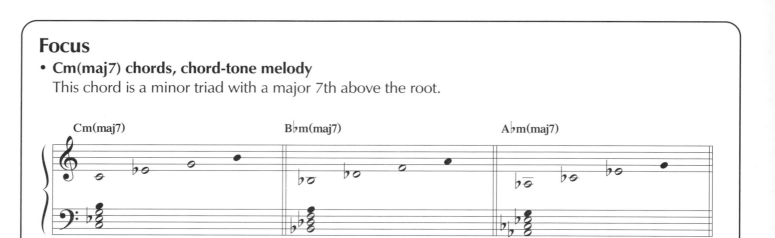

Listen Up

Medium swing ($\quad$ = ca. 108)

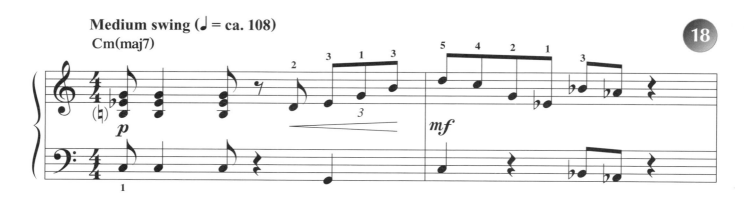

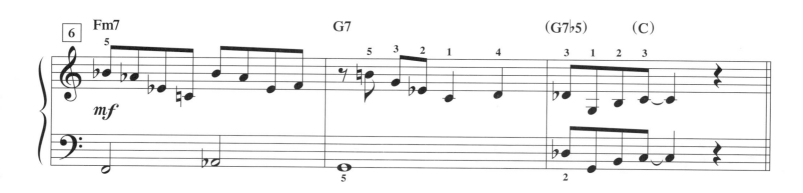

Learning To Read Slash Chord Symbols

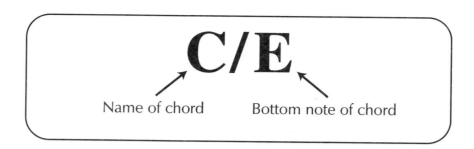

Slash chords look like this:

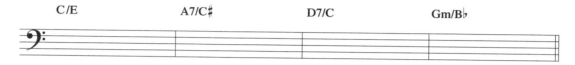

Slash chords sound like this:

Lead sheet with slash chords

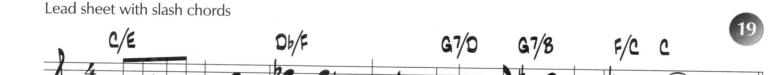

Actual performance of lead sheet with slash chords

From lead sheet to performance

Warm-up practice sequence

Step 1: Play chords as written.

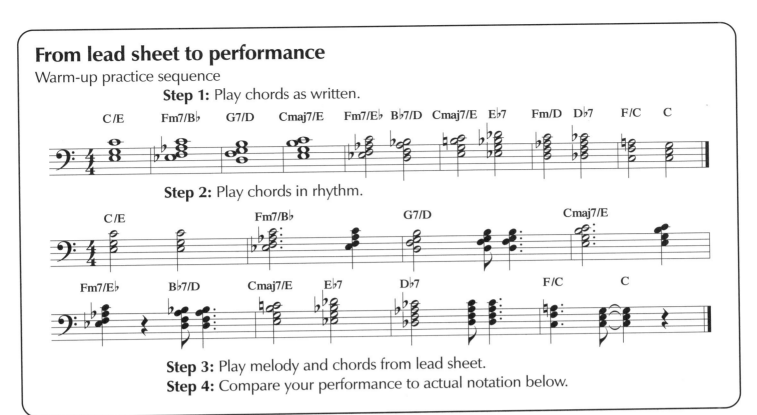

Step 2: Play chords in rhythm.

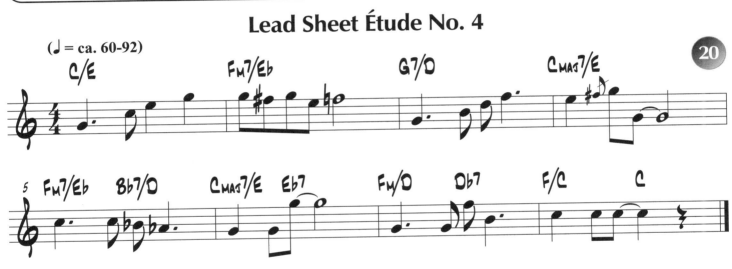

Step 3: Play melody and chords from lead sheet.
Step 4: Compare your performance to actual notation below.

Lead Sheet Étude No. 4

Actual notation of *Lead Sheet Étude No. 4*

Write & Play

Write in the notes of the L.H. chords in the empty measures below, using the chord symbols as a guide.
Then play this jazz ballad slowly and sensitively.

Shadows of the Past

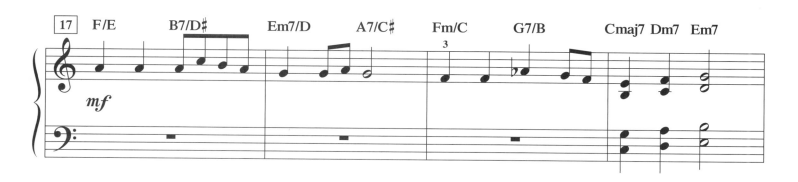

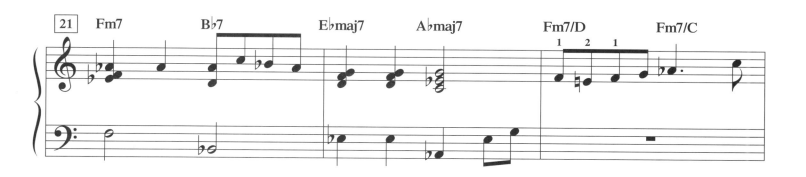

FJH1348

Part 3: Basic Jazz Repertoire—The Standards*

Fake Book

The standards are most often found in "fake books." In these books, lead sheets are presented with the melody (R.H.) and the chord symbols (L.H.).

Part III offers a preparation sequence for each hand so that a full performance of the lead sheet may be performed with ease. Each of the performance lead sheets contains a bit of standard notation for both hands to play, including a written improvisation.

Preparing the R.H.

     1. Accents—Apply jazz basic and swing accents as indicated.
     2. Memorize and proceed to page 39.

When the Saints Go Marching In
(lead sheet)

Traditional

22

Standards—Jazz music that has remained popular over a long period of time. Learning to play jazz includes learning these classic compositions.

Preparing the L.H.

1. Walking bass

Write and play the following for all C chords (measures 1–4, 9–10, and 15–16):

2. Single tone

Write and play the following for the G chord (measures 7–8)

and the F chord (measure 11):

3. 2-note chord

Write and play the following 2-note chords in all the remaining measures, using the suggested rhythms (♩ notes).

When the Saints Go Marching In
(L.H. application)

4. Play hands together!

Performance

Play either a (1) walking bass, (2) single-note bass, or (3) 2-note chord in the empty measures below.
Practice slowly until you can perform the fully notated sections and the lead sheet section at the same tempo.

When the Saints Go Marching In

Traditional
Arr. Konowitz

Fake Book

Preparing the L.H.

1. Play single notes from slash chords.

Bill Bailey, Won't You Please Come Home?

2. Write and play the chords below, using this rhythm:

Performance

Measures 5–16—Play single notes (from slash chords) in the empty measures below.

Measures 21–34—Play L.H. chords in the empty measures below, using the chord symbols and suggested rhythms practiced on page 42.

Bill Bailey, Won't You Please Come Home?

Traditional
Arr. Konowitz

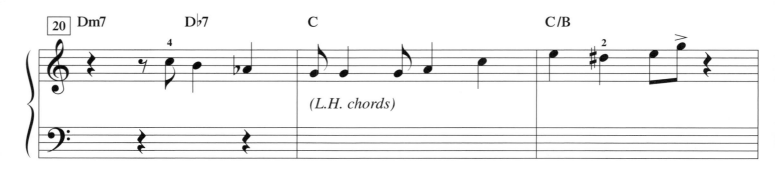

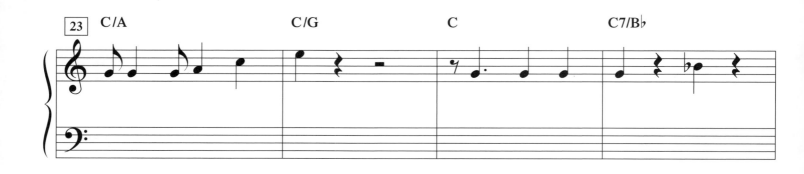

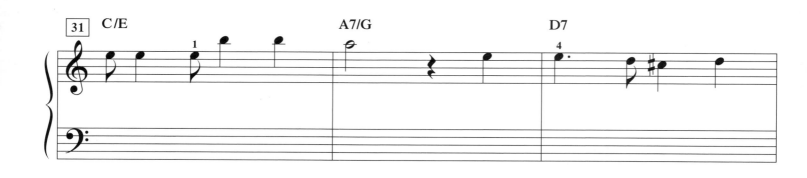

Optional: On beat 3, say, "Bill Bailey, please come home!"

The St. Louis Blues
(performance)

W.C. Handy
Arr. Konowitz